A Raindrop's Journey

by Suzanne Slade

illustrated by Holli Conger

PICTURE WINDOW BOOKS
a capstone imprint

Thanks to our advisers for their expertise, research, and advice:

Virg Debban, Secondary Science Teacher (ret.)
New Ulm (Minnesota) Public Schools, ISD 88

Terry Flaherty, PhD, Professor of English
Minnesota State University, Mankato

Editor: Jill Kalz
Designer: Tracy Davies
Art Director: Nathan Gassman
Production Specialist: Sarah Bennett
The illustrations in this book were created with mixed media/found object.

Picture Window Books
151 Good Counsel Drive
P.O. Box 669
Mankato, MN 56002-0669
877-845-8392
www.capstonepub.com

All books published by Picture Window Books are manufactured
with paper containing at least 10 percent post-consumer waste.

Library of Congress Cataloging-in-Publication Data
Slade, Suzanne.
  A raindrop's journey / by Suzanne Slade ; illustrated by Holli Conger.
     p. cm. — (Follow it!)
  Includes index.
  ISBN 978-1-4048-6266-1 (library binding)
  ISBN 978-1-4048-6712-3 (paperback)
  1. Hydrologic cycle—Juvenile literature. 2. Raindrops—Juvenile
literature. I. Conger, Holli, ill. II. Title.
  GB848.S56 2011
  551.48—dc22   2010033772

Printed in the United States of America in North Mankato, Minnesota.
092010
005933CGS11

Rumble! Crash! Boom!

Dark, angry clouds gather. Lightning streaks across the sky.

But in the middle of this large storm, something very small—and very special—is happening too.

A raindrop begins to form.

Hang on! This is just the beginning!

ICE CRYSTALS

WATER VAPOR

DUST

Clouds are made of small ice crystals, water vapor, and very tiny bits of dust. A droplet forms when water vapor gathers around a bit of dust and condenses. When many droplets join together, they form rain, snow, or other kinds of precipitation.

Drip! Drip! Drop!

The water drop hurtles toward Earth with thousands of other raindrops. A bright ray of sunlight shines through the drops and creates a beautiful rainbow.

Hey, guys! Look what we made!

Plop!

The raindrop lands on smooth rock.

It trickles down the hill and joins millions of other drops in a small stream. The stream twists, turns, winds, and wanders. Then it empties into a wide river.

Rol-lin'. Rol-lin'. Rol-lin' down the ri-ver!

Most rainwater soaks into the ground. Plants then draw out the water with their roots. During transpiration, this liquid water turns into water vapor. The vapor escapes through small holes in the plants' leaves called stomata. A large oak tree puts about 40,000 gallons (151,000 liters) of water vapor into the air every year!

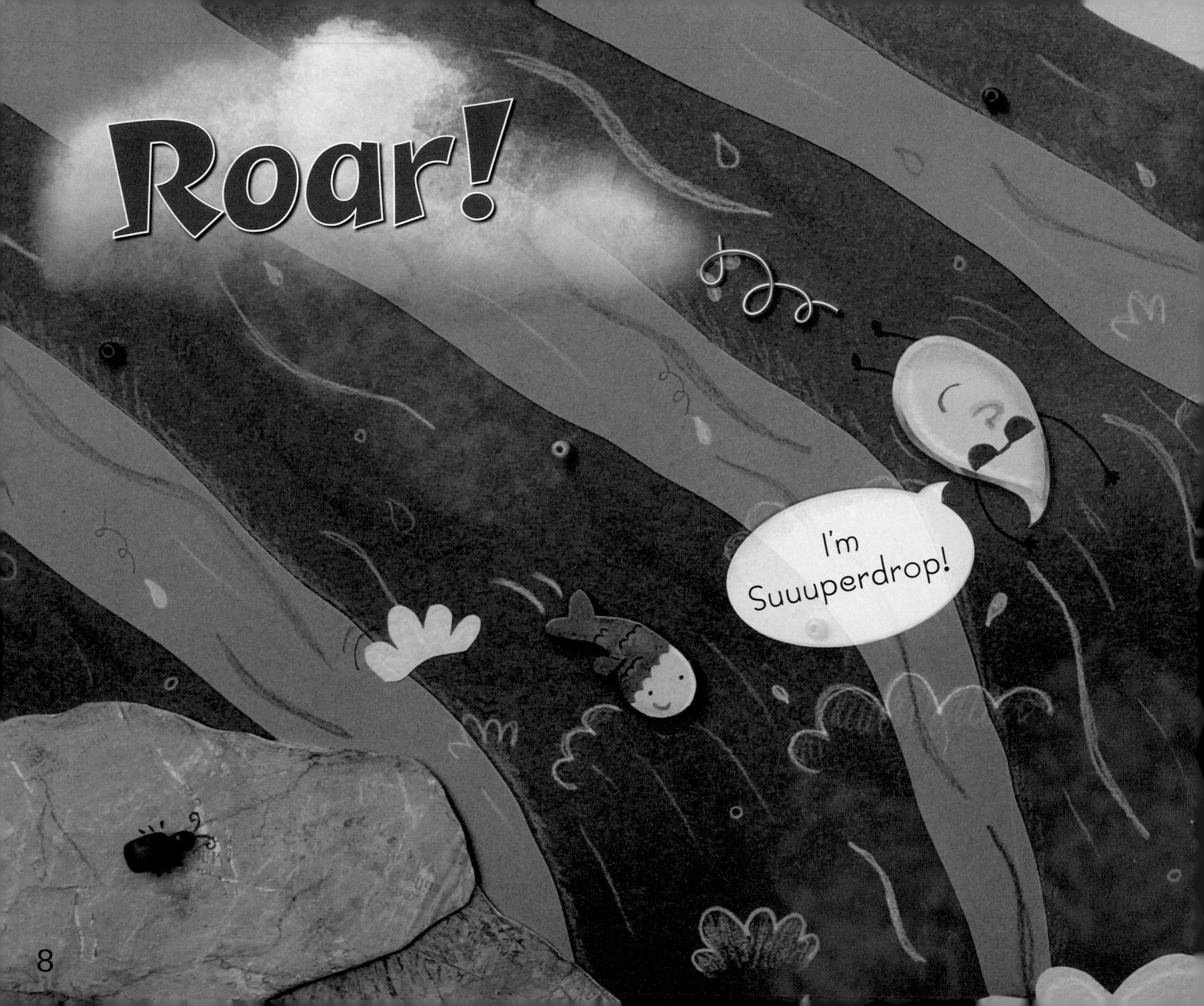
Roar!
I'm Suuuperdrop!

The drop doesn't even see what's coming next.
It soars over the edge of a rocky cliff ...
and becomes part of an amazing waterfall!

9

Splash!

The drop makes a
spectacular landing.

It bounces across the
churning water ...

10

9

8

... then flows into a huge, peaceful lake.

But the drop doesn't rest there for long.

About 70 percent of Earth's surface is covered by water. Only 1 percent of that is freshwater people can use. Most of Earth's water is stored in salty oceans or frozen inside huge glaciers.

Ahh ... Time to kick back and relax.

11

... to a tall tower.

Now the drop must wait.
But what is it waiting for?

Once the drop's squeaky
clean, it moves through
another pipe up, up, up ...

In the United States, the
average person uses more
than 100 gallons (379 liters)
of water every day.

13

Burble. Gurgle.

Finally, the long wait is over.

The drop flows through lots of smaller pipes—up, down, all around—and into a house.

Pshhhhht!
The drop gushes out of a faucet and lands in a glass.
Uncle Drip! Where've you been?
Hi, Squirt! Oh, just chillin' in the freezer.

Gulp, gulp, gulp!

A big, thirsty mouth drinks the drop right down.

Everything turns dark. Then the drop feels hot. Hotter. And hotter still.

Suddenly it pops through the boy's skin, onto his forehead!

Sweat!

Whoa. That was an amazing trip!

Your body is mostly water—about 60 percent. Drinking water is important for good health.

Splat!

The drop falls off the boy's face and lands on the hot pavement below. In the blazing sunlight, the drop starts to feel strange. VERY strange.

The sun's heat turns the drop into water vapor. The warm water vapor drifts over the boy, above the house, and into the wide, open sky.

The sun powers the water cycle. Every day its rays heat up millions of gallons of water in rivers, lakes, and oceans, creating water vapor. The process of a liquid turning into gas is called evaporation.

I'm here. I'm there. I'm everywhere!

The water vapor gathers in a cloud and condenses into a droplet. A strong wind pushes the cloud northward. The air gets colder, and the water drop begins to feel strange again.

Then something truly amazing happens—the drop changes into a snowflake!

The snowflake floats to Earth, ready to start another exciting journey in the water cycle.

Since Earth began, the same water has moved through the air, oceans, plants, and even people in the water cycle. The water in your bathtub may have once been ice at the top of Mount Everest!

Diagram of a Raindrop's Journey

cloud

raindrop

stream

lake

waterfall

river

water treatment plant

water tower

drinking glass

sweat

snowflakes

droplets

water vapor

Glossary

condense—to change from a gas to a liquid; the process is called condensation

evaporation—the process of changing from a liquid to a gas

glacier—a large slow-moving body of ice

precipitation—water that falls from the clouds in the form of rain, hail, or snow

transpiration—the process of water moving through a plant from its roots to the air

water cycle—the endless movement of water as it falls to the earth as precipitation and rises up again as water vapor

water vapor—water in a gas form

To Learn More

More Books to Read

Bauman, Amy. *Earth's Water Cycle.* Planet Earth. Pleasantville, N.Y.: Gareth Stevens Pub., 2008.
Blackaby, Susan. *Water Wise.* Read-It! Readers. Science. Minneapolis: Picture Window Books, 2009.
Korb, Rena. *The Wild Water Cycle.* Science Rocks! Edina, Minn.: Magic Wagon, 2008.

Internet Sites

FactHound offers a safe, fun way to find Internet sites related to this book. All of the sites on FactHound have been researched by our staff.

Here's all you do:
Visit *www.facthound.com*
Type in this code: 9781404862661

Super-cool stuff!

Check out projects, games and lots more at
www.capstonekids.com

Index

Look for all the books in the Follow It series:

A Dollar Bill's Journey

A Germ's Journey

A Plastic Bottle's Journey

A Raindrop's Journey